All about you

Who are your family?

Jillian Powell

Wayland

All about you

Where did you come from?
Who are you?
Who are your family?
Who are your friends?

Picture acknowledgements

The publishers would like to thank the following for allowing their photographs to be reproduced in this book: Chris Fairclough Picture Library 5 (above), 6 (above), 12, 19 (below), 21 (below); Chapel Studios 9 (below); Reflections (Jennie Woodcock) 7, 9 (above), 16, 19 (above), 25; Skjold 17 (below); Wayland Picture Library 8, 14 (below), 15 (above); Tim Woodcock 21 (above), 23 (below), 29; ZEFA cover, 4, 5 (below), 7, 10, 11, 14 (above), 17 (above), 18 (both), 20, 22, 23 (above), 27, 28.

Series editor: Francesca Motisi
Editor: Joan Walters
Series designer: Jean Wheeler

This edition published in 1996 by
Wayland (Publishers) Ltd

First published in 1993 by
Wayland (Publishers) Limited
61, Western Road, Hove
East Sussex, BN3 1JD England

© Copyright 1993 Wayland (Publishers) Limited

British Library Cataloguing in Publication Data
Powell, Jillian
Who are your family? – (All About You Series)
I. Title   II. Series
306.85

HARDBACK ISBN 0-7502-0790-6

PAPERBACK ISBN 0-7502-1891-6

Typeset by Dorchester Typesetting Group Limited
Printed and bound by Rotolito Lombarda S.p.A., Milan, Italy

Contents

When you were born you became part of a
   family   4

Your family may be you and your mum or dad   6

Sometimes, big families live together   8

If you live with one parent, you may spend
   some days with your other parent   10

You may live with foster parents   12

Who else is in your family?   14

Families can grow   16

It can be fun doing things together as a family 18

Families can share work   20

Living as a family you get to know each other 22

Sometimes, you may quarrel   24

You can tell your family if you are unhappy   26

People in families may give each other
   presents   28

Notes for parents and teachers   30

Topic web   31

Glossary   32

Books to read and Index   32

When you were born, you
became part of a family.

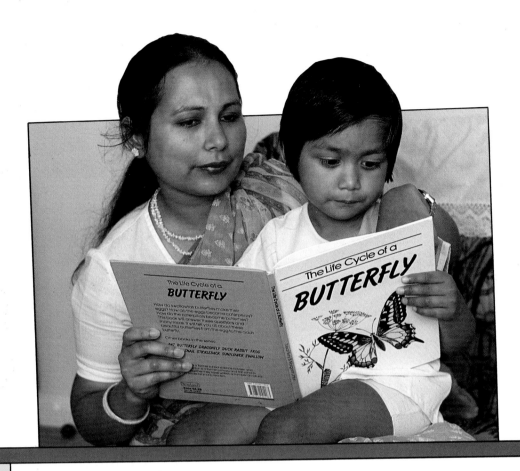

Families are different sizes.
Who are your family?

Your family
may be you
and your
mum or dad.

Just two people can live together as a family.

Sometimes, big families live together, with mum, dad, children and one or more grandparents.

Younger members
of the family
may look after
grandparents
when they are
old or need care.

You can have
fun with
grandparents too.

If you live with one of your parents, you may spend weekends or holidays with your other parent.

If your mum or dad marries
again, you will have a stepdad
or stepmum and maybe
stepbrothers and stepsisters.

You may live with **foster** parents. They are not your birth parents but they love and care for you.

Perhaps you have brothers or sisters in your family.

Who else is in your family?
You may have grandparents,
aunts, uncles and cousins.

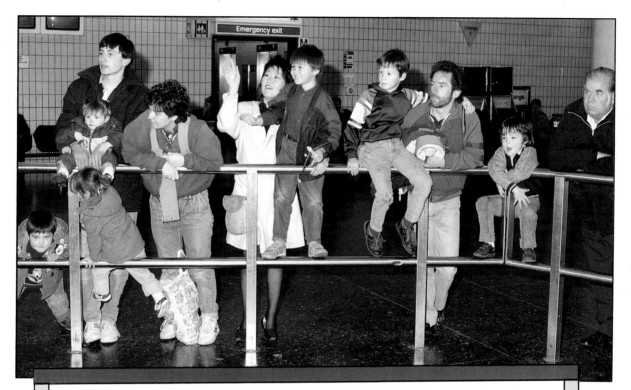

Some of your family may live near you, and others far away.

It is fun when they come to visit but sad to say goodbye.

Families can grow. Your family
will grow if your parents have
a new baby.

If they **adopt** or foster another child, you will have a new brother or sister.

17

It can be fun doing things together as a family.

Think of some of the things you do together.

Perhaps you like going for a walk, sharing meals, or playing games with your family?

Families can share work too and help each other around the home.

Everyone can join in with laying the table, or helping Mum or Dad with the washing.

Living as a family, you get to know each other very well. You know when someone in your family is happy.

You also know when someone is sad, angry, hurt or ill, You can help each other feel better.

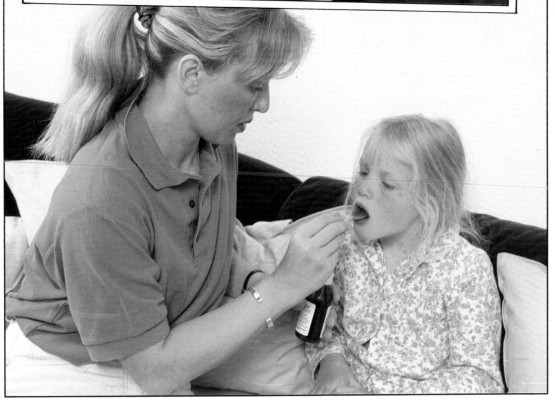

Sometimes, you may **quarrel** with someone in your family. It doesn't mean you stop loving one another.

It's good to make up and be friends again.

You can tell someone in your family if you are unhappy or frightened about something. Talking about it can help you feel better.

It is also good to share happy feelings.

People in families may give each other presents on special days like birthdays.

Giving small presents or treats is one way of showing that you love and care for each other.

Notes for parents and teachers

Maths
● Number: Children could add up the ages of all their family members; put these in order; work out the lowest, highest, median and average (using a calculator). Similarly, they could work out the ages in months and years of their classmates and put these in order.
● The idea of a 'family' of objects is a good starting point for sorting and sets work.
● Data handling: Number of family members could be expressed in a block graph. Make-up of the family – brothers and sisters or neither – could be expressed using mapping, as a Venn diagram, or (using a computer programme) Pie Chart.
● Enter and access data on computer database e.g. 'Our facts'.

Language
● Family albums can be made using photographs and pictures with some information about each member: 'This is a photo of my Auntie Jean – she is kind to me and buys me clothes' etc. Family members (especially grandmothers and grandfathers) can be interviewed about *their* parents.
● Family rituals can be collected: 'Every Saturday afternoon we have cakes for tea'; 'On Wednesdays we all go swimming'.
● Word families: A good opportunity to discuss and collect words which have similar spelling patterns and also similar *types* of words i.e. the parts of speech: 'doing words', 'describing words' etc.
● The writing of letters to family members who live far away.

Science
● An investigation into inherited characteristics such as eye colour, hair texture/colour, whether one can 'fold' one's tongue etc., might involve interviewing family members to discover patterns of inheritance.
● Animal families: a) as a means of genetic classification e.g. the cat family; the ape family; the crow family; the rodent family etc. b) the proper names for male/female/young of a species: cow, bull, calf, pen, cob, cygnet etc.

Geography
● Studies could be made of families from different cultures and countries around the world. Comparisons and contrasts could be made with the lifestyle of their own families.
● Those children who have relatives living in other countries could write to them. These locations could be pinned on a map of the world.

Technology
● Children could design and build a model, using junk materials, of a suitable shelter for themselves and their families, for life on another planet e.g. Mars.

History
● Famous families in history (and Literature): Brontë sisters; Grace Darling; The Curies; Swiss Family Robinson; Happy Families (Ahlbergs); Goldilocks and the Three Bears.
● Study and contrast a family from a different era e.g. Viking; Egyptian; Greek; Victorian etc. Write 'A Day in the Life' as a family member of one of these.

Art and Craft
● Family mobiles: to include grandparents and even pets; these can be hung in the classroom to show how families differ.
● Colour families: primary colours; 'warm' colours and 'cold' colours; colours which give distance (e.g. blue) to a picture and colours (e.g. red) that bring things nearer ; colours which 'go' well with one another and those that don't; mixing paints etc.

P.E./Dance/Drama
● Small groups of children can be given an animal family e.g. the cat family; they could explore and negotiate apparatus as members of this family.
● Similarly, children could be asked to work out a dance for a given animal family e.g. the dance of the whale family.
● Drama: acting out in small groups a family scene e.g. breakfast time – late for school; an argument over what television programme to watch.

Music
● Songs that have 'families' as a theme e.g. 'The Family of Man'.
● Musical instrument families: brass, woodwind, plucked, orchestral etc.

Multicultural/R.E./Health
● An investigation into children's relations living in other countries (see Geography) and the cultural traditions alive within their immediate families.
● What the expression 'The Family of Man' might mean.
● How 'families' are featured in various religions: the family of Gods; families in religious stories e.g. the prodigal son.
● Noah's Ark: Noah's family and the animal families – two by two.

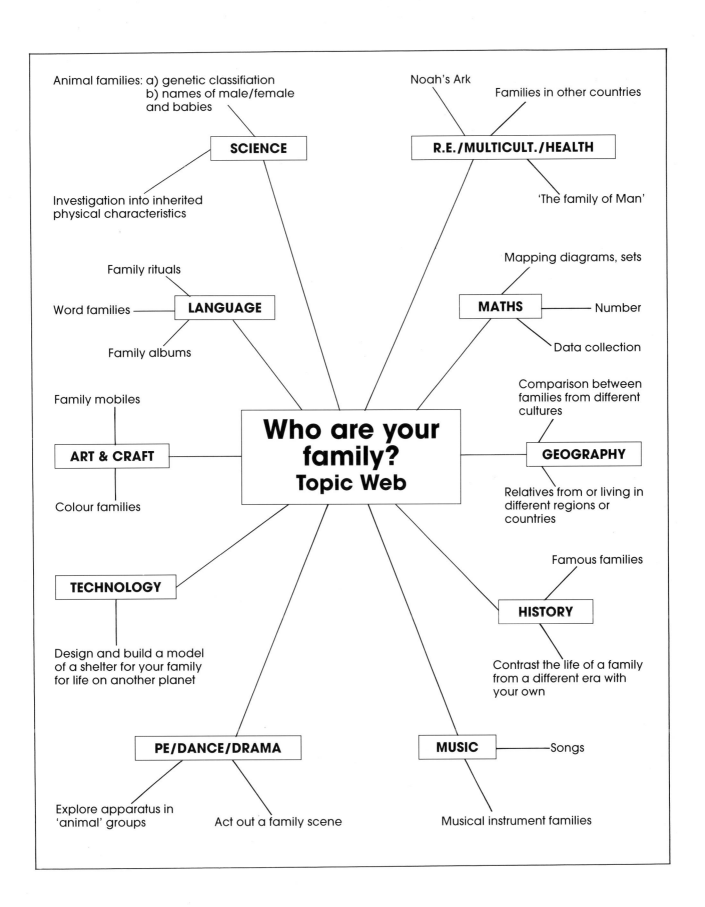

Animal families: a) genetic classifiation
b) names of male/female and babies

SCIENCE

Investigation into inherited physical characteristics

Noah's Ark

Families in other countries

R.E./MULTICULT./HEALTH

'The family of Man'

Family rituals

Word families —

LANGUAGE

Family albums

Mapping diagrams, sets

MATHS — Number

Data collection

Family mobiles

ART & CRAFT

Colour families

Comparison between families from different cultures

GEOGRAPHY

Relatives from or living in different regions or countries

Who are your family?
Topic Web

TECHNOLOGY

Design and build a model of a shelter for your family for life on another planet

Famous families

HISTORY

Contrast the life of a family from a different era with your own

PE/DANCE/DRAMA

Explore apparatus in 'animal' groups

Act out a family scene

MUSIC — Songs

Musical instrument families

Glossary

Adopt   To bring up someone else's child as your own and to love and care for that child.

Foster   To look after someone else's child for a while, and to make them feel at home in your family until a home can be found where that child can stay

Quarrel   An argument.

Index

Adopt 17

Baby 16
Brothers 13, 17

Cousins 14

Dad 6, 8, 11

Foster 17
Foster parents 12

Grandparents 8, 9, 14

Mum 6, 8, 11

Quarrel 24

Sharing feelings 26, 27
Sisters 13, 17
Stepbrothers 11
Stepdad 11
Stepmum 11
Stepsisters 11

Uncles 14

Books to read

Your World Series: Your Family by Michael Pollard (Wayland 1989)

My Family by Kati Teague (Macdonald 1988)

Children Need Families by Michael Pollard (Wayland 1988)

Family Life by B. McConville (Macdonald 1988)